I0054081

W∅W

Choosing a
Career as a
Paralegal

Paralegals assist lawyers in preparing cases. If you are interested in the legal system, a career as a paralegal may be right for you.

WAW

Choosing a Career as a Paralegal

Holly Cefrey

The Rosen Publishing Group, Inc.
New York

To my family

Published in 2001 by The Rosen Publishing Group, Inc.
29 East 21st Street, New York, NY 10010

Copyright © 2001 by The Rosen Publishing Group, Inc.

Revised Edition 2001

All rights reserved. No part of this book may be reproduced in any form without permission in writing from the publisher, except by a reviewer.

Library of Congress Cataloging-in-Publication Data

Cefrey, Holly.
Choosing a career as a paralegal / by Holly Cefrey.
p. cm. — (The world of work)
Includes bibliographical references and index.
ISBN 978-1-4358-8668-1
1. Legal assistants—Vocational guidance—United States. [1. Legal assistants—Vocational guidance. 2. Vocational guidance.] I. Title. II. World of work (New York, N.Y.)
KF320.L4 C44 2001
340'.023'73—dc21

00-013130

Manufactured in the United States of America

Contents

WᎯW

Introduction

*O*ur class took a field trip to the city courthouse. At the very least, I was excited to be getting out of school for the day. The courthouse is one of the oldest buildings in our city. There were many people touring the courthouse, but there were also a number of people who were there to work. While waiting to enter one of the courtrooms, I watched people come and go. Some people were there to pay fines, some to appear in court, and some to get married. I watched a local television reporter interview an attorney who came out of one of the courtrooms. I was surprised to see how many different things go on at the city courthouse in a day.

We watched a case about a newly married couple who were suing their wedding photographer. Although the pictures the photographer had taken of the couple's wedding day were blurry, she refused to refund their money. The couple had spent a small fortune on the wedding, including money for the photographer's services. They had hoped *the photos would document their special day. The couple was suing not only for a refund but also for money to make up for the memories lost to bad photographs. The photographer's lawyer said that the photographer had created blurry photographs on purpose; it was an artistic statement. The couple's lawyer said that the photographer took photographs that looked nothing like her portfolio photos or advertisement. Their lawyer went on to say that the law required the photographer to provide services as promised or advertised and that the photographer had failed to do so.*

Throughout the trial, a legal assistant helped the couple's lawyer. This legal assistant, also known as a paralegal, wrote down notes as the lawyer whispered to him. He shuffled through papers and handed information back to the lawyer. It seemed that the lawyer relied on the assistant quite a bit, and they worked well as a team. The couple won their case. The court awarded them a refund and additional money to make up for the stress and problems that the photographer had caused.

Of all the people I observed that day, the paralegal seemed to have the most rewarding job. I learned that paralegals are valuable team members. They research important information and help lawyers present their cases to the courts. Paralegals watch the legal system in action and see their work pay off when their team wins a case. And each case is different, so there are always new people and new challenges.

—Trini, age sixteen

What Trini describes is our legal system. The legal system is made up of laws and the people who make, interpret, and enforce those laws. Laws are rules that direct people's behaviors. Ideally, these laws establish order and protect us from harming others and ourselves. The hope is that if a society makes and enforces these rules, every person will have a clear idea of what behaviors are acceptable.

Rule Makers

Politicians create many new laws each year. A law begins as a bill brought before the United States Congress. Laws are not physical objects; they are ideas put into words. Schoolteachers, parents, community leaders, and many others teach people about laws and the importance of following them. Also, since laws are ideas, they can be interpreted in many ways. People working in the legal system not only enforce but also try to define, or explain, the meaning of laws and how they should be followed.

Rule Breakers

Punishment is another key aspect of our legal system. A person is punished if he or she breaks the law. The hope is that if a person is punished, he or she will be less likely to break the law again. Punishments for breaking the law range from fines and community service to jail time and, in some cases, death.

The law guarantees that every person has the right to have a lawyer. A lawyer, also called an attorney, is a law specialist. Lawyers are legal professionals who have education, training, and experience in understanding law. They can use their knowledge of law to do two things: defend or prosecute. Lawyers can defend their clients from punishment. They can also prosecute, or bring punishment to those who break the law. Many lawyers use a team of people to help them research and present their cases. One of the most valuable team members is the paralegal.

Questions to Ask Yourself

Does the idea of understanding laws and the legal system interest you? Do you enjoy working with different people? Do you find the idea of spending hours preparing for a case interesting or exciting? Would you rather be a lawyer, who argues a case, or a paralegal, who helps to prepare the case?

A lawyer is hired to represent a person with a legal problem in court.

1

Law and the Paralegal

Often a person with a legal problem seeks the help of a lawyer. After listening to the problem, the lawyer decides whether or not to take the case. If the lawyer takes the case, it becomes the lawyer's job to understand all of the specific details about the case. The lawyer researches similar cases in the past that won in court. By using past case examples, the lawyer hopes to persuade the judge or jury to rule in favor of his or her client. The lawyer also needs to make sure that he or she knows all the details or facts about a case. The lawyer arranges interviews with the people involved to uncover all the facts of a case.

When the case goes to court, the lawyer argues on behalf of the client. He or she presents the case to the court. The lawyer calls witnesses to help support the points of the case. The opposing lawyer presents his or her side of the case, calling his or her own witnesses. After receiving information from lawyers, clients, and witnesses, a judge or a jury rule on the case, deciding in favor of one side or the other.

Pulling It Together

As you can tell, a lawyer must perform many tasks in order to prepare for court. These tasks require special knowledge of laws and the legal process. A single task often demands a lawyer's total attention. Nonetheless, other tasks must be done. This is when a lawyer hires a legal assistant, or paralegal. The term "legal assistant" has the same meaning as the word "paralegal." While people use the term "legal assistant" quite often, professional paralegal associations prefer to use the term "paralegal." A paralegal is allowed by law to help with some of the lawyer's tasks. A lawyer always supervises and directs a paralegal.

People drawn to the paralegal profession have a strong interest in the law. They understand the importance of completing very involved research and enjoy doing such work. Paralegals must solve problems in both practical and creative ways. In many cases, the paralegal is the person who helps pull all of the facts or details of a case together.

Paralegal Work

When preparing cases, paralegals often perform some of the same tasks as a lawyer. Paralegals often work hand in hand with a lawyer to prepare a case for trial. As a paralegal gains more work experience, the number of tasks given to the paralegal increases. What makes a paralegal different from a clerk or secretary is that paralegals perform specific legal tasks. Lawyers do not pass these tasks on to secretaries or clerks. If

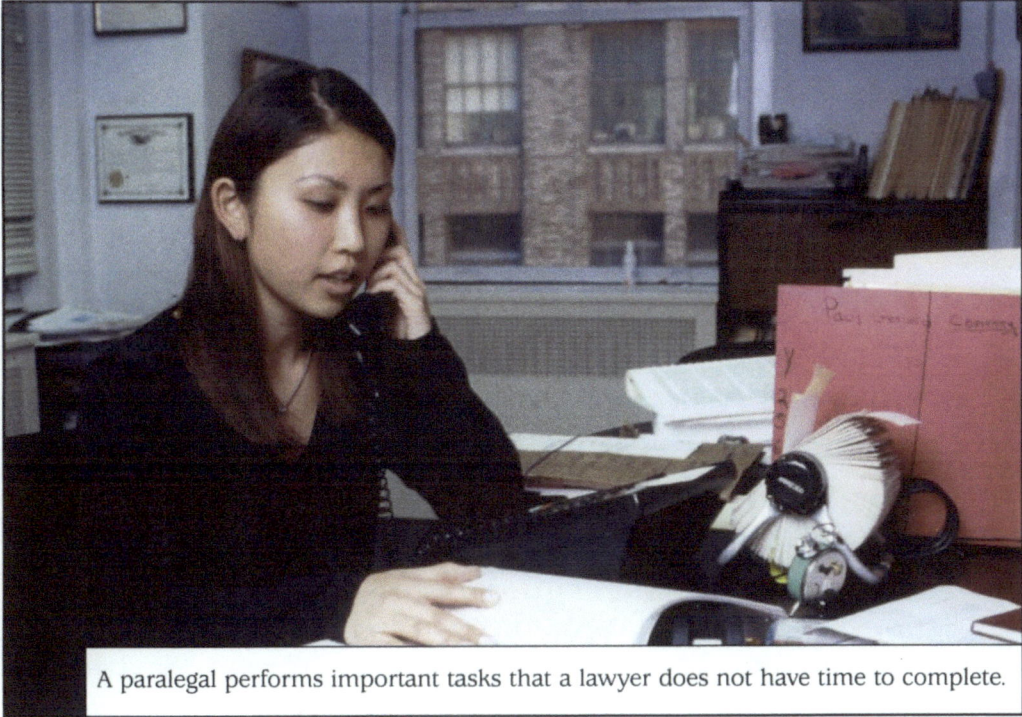

A paralegal performs important tasks that a lawyer does not have time to complete.

a paralegal is not working on a case, the lawyer performs these duties.

Defining the Boundaries

There are some ways in which working as a paralegal differs from working as a lawyer.

- ✔ Paralegals cannot practice law.
- ✔ Paralegals are not allowed to give legal advice.
- ✔ Paralegals are not allowed to present or to try a case in court.
- ✔ Paralegals are not allowed to set or accept legal fees.
- ✔ Paralegals cannot accept or reject clients.

Lawyers are educated, trained, and licensed to practice law. As licensed law specialists, they are allowed to give legal advice. Lawyers can set and accept legal fees as well as accept or reject clients. Fees for the work that a paralegal does for a lawyer are added to the lawyer's total bill. Finally, only lawyers are allowed to present or to try a case in court.

Paralegal Duties

In addition to research and paperwork, the paralegal interacts with the client and other people involved with the case. The relationship between the client, the paralegal, and the lawyer must remain clearly defined. The client must be informed that the paralegal is acting on behalf of the lawyer and is acting under the direction of a lawyer. Before a paralegal can become involved with the client, the client must be fully aware that the paralegal is not a lawyer but a legal assistant. For a given case, the duties of a paralegal might include:

✔ Researching library and government records for past legal decisions that affect the current case

✔ Reviewing law books for laws that support the case

✔ Recording all the details or facts of the case

✔ Filing the appropriate paperwork for court proceedings

✔ Conducting interviews with clients

Paralegals frequently research past legal decisions.

✔ Maintaining contact with the client, providing the client with updates about the case

✔ Locating and interviewing possible witnesses

✔ Writing reports for the lawyer about research and investigative findings

✔ Drafting documents or papers that the lawyer will use during the case or legal proceedings

✔ Organizing the files and facts of each case for quick and easy reference

✔ Attending court proceedings or other meetings with the lawyer

✔ Assisting the lawyer during the trial

Paralegals who work in law firms or with a lawyer may have office duties as well. Tasks can vary, depending on the individual needs of the employer. Paralegals may also:

✔ Organize the activities of other law firm employees

✔ Organize and maintain the law firm's financial files

✔ Organize files on law guidelines and reference materials

✔ Read and interpret information for law firm use

Several organizations, bar associations, legislatures, and courts have defined the responsibilities of a paralegal. The National Association of Legal Assistants Inc. has evaluated these definitions and combined their common elements in order to create a simplified version. A paralegal is a person who:

✔ Has received special training through formal education or through many years of experience

✔ Works under the supervision and direction of an attorney

✔ Performs nonclerical and nonsecretarial legal work in assisting an attorney

Some paralegals attend formal paralegal training programs; others become paralegals after working many years for a lawyer. Some paralegals have an educational background in another area that led them into legal work. For example, a person working as an environmentalist might switch careers to become a paralegal. This former environmentalist could assist a lawyer who specializes in environmental law. The person is hired because he or she already knows about environmental issues, and he or she is trained to do paralegal work relating to environmental law.

Working with People

In an average day, a paralegal comes into contact with a variety of people. Being a "people person" is definitely a job requirement. Paralegals must be able to be team players. In addition to working with the lawyer and the client, paralegals must work with secretaries, proofreaders, and judicial clerks.

One might think that the close supervision of a lawyer would prevent a paralegal from working independently. This is entirely untrue. Most lawyers set boundaries but then allow their paralegals to operate on their own within those boundaries. Paralegals use independent and creative thinking to understand and interpret events of a case and the laws that pertain to a case. They also prepare a case for trial. Paralegals spend many unsupervised work hours at a desk in an office or at a law library.

Questions to Ask Yourself

Are you a team player? Do you enjoy interacting with other people? Can you get things done when left on your own? Do you enjoy reading and trying to understand detailed cases? Do you like to solve problems? Do you like to organize things?

2

Employment as a Paralegal

While paralegal work is very specific, paralegals can have varied educational and professional backgrounds. They can also specialize in an area of law that most interests them. Many different kinds of offices benefit from the help that paralegals provide.

A History of the Profession

"Paralegal" is a relatively new word. People began to use the word "paralegal" in the early 1970s to describe a person who assisted an attorney. The actual use of paralegals, known then as legal assistants, dates back to the 1960s.

During his 1964 State of the Union Address, President Lyndon Johnson declared an "unconditional war on poverty." The nation responded with federal, private, and local, or grassroots, programs. Public agencies began to hire individuals to help those lawyers who made their services available to

The civil rights movement of the 1960s brought about a greater awareness of the legal system and increased lawyers' workloads.

the poor. Because assistants took over tasks formerly performed by lawyers, the use of these assistants reduced the amount of time and money spent on each case. Lawyers could then help a greater number of clients.

Additionally, reform efforts, such as the civil rights movement, brought about a greater awareness of the legal system and its uses for the general public. Law firms and independent lawyers experienced a surge in caseloads and needed help. In addition to government agencies, law firms and independent lawyers started hiring assistants to help manage their heavy workloads.

By 1971, there were approximately ten paralegal training programs in the United States. Before this time, most paralegals trained on the job. Today, there are over 650 programs or schools that provide paralegal training in the United States. Once trained, paralegals can work in a variety of places.

Possible Employers

Paralegals are not limited to working for a lawyer or a law firm. Paralegals can work in many other places where people perform law-related work. Paralegals can also work on a freelance basis, which means that they work for different employers for short periods of time. Some paralegals start their own businesses, providing services for any number of offices. Examples of places where paralegals work are:

- ✔ Accounting firms

- ✔ Banks

Several popular television programs, including *The Practice*, dramatize working in the legal profession.

✔ Construction companies

✔ Corporations

✔ Courts

✔ Engineering firms

✔ Government agencies

✔ Individual lawyers

✔ Insurance agencies

✔ Legal aid clinics

✔ Private law firms

✔ Real estate agencies

The Three Most Common Employers

Private law firms, corporations, and government agencies employ the greatest number of paralegals. Most employers in these areas have a staff of several paralegals working on many cases. These paralegals usually work the standard forty-hour work week. In the event of a tight deadline, or if there is a dramatic increase in the number of cases handled by an office, the paralegal staff will work longer hours. Many employers reward paralegals who work overtime with bonuses or paid time off from work.

Law Firms

A law firm is a group of two or more lawyers who operate as one business. Paralegals working in law firms perform a wide variety of tasks. These jobs require a broad knowledge of the law because many firms handle many different kinds of cases, from settling a divorce or composing a real estate contract to defending a person accused of murder. Paralegals at law firms conduct the research and interviews for each case. Additionally, they may write reports, analyze legal documents, and prepare paperwork and legal forms. Also, they sometimes assist lawyers in the courtroom.

Corporations

A corporation is a legal or business organization consisting of many individuals who agree to operate as a single unit with a common goal. Corporate paralegals are involved in the organization's business operations. They come to

Most lawyers, like the members of the "Dream Team" in the O. J. Simpson trial, specialize in a specific area of law.

understand the corporation's goals, products, and structure as insiders. Most corporate paralegals write business agreements and employee contracts. They are involved in writing employee benefit, shareholder, and stock option plans. Corporate paralegals also review government regulations to make sure that the corporation operates legally.

Government Offices

Many government agencies employ paralegals. Paralegals work for the Departments of Justice, Treasury, and Defense. They also work at the White House. Government paralegals find and evaluate evidence and manage hearings. Government paralegals also maintain reference files and answer questions about government laws and regulations.

Paralegals can work for state and local government agencies as well. Government paralegals working on the state and local levels perform legal duties relating to a variety of issues, such as welfare, health care, landlord/tenant relations, unemployment, and social security.

If it weren't for paralegals, we could never handle the caseload that we have. We are a pretty small firm; there are four lawyers here, including myself. Having a staff of paralegals helps us to take on more cases. Taking on more cases is good for our firm because it brings in more money and helps get the name of the firm out there. The specialized training that paralegals have allows lawyers to practice law and not get too bogged down in research. They save us from having to do a huge amount of important but time-consuming groundwork.
—Barbara Haley, lawyer

Choosing a Specialty

Most lawyers focus their practice in a particular area of the law; they become specialists. For example, a lawyer interested in laws relating to divorce would become a divorce attorney and accept only divorce cases. The same can be said for paralegals. Paralegals choose a particular area of law on which to focus. If a paralegal is interested in laws concerning building and

A paralegal who specializes in tax law might work for a large corporation.

construction, he or she would most likely work for a construction company.

These areas of specialization include but are not limited to:

✔ Copyright law

✔ Criminal law

✔ Employment law

✔ Family law

✔ Health care

✔ Housing law

✔ Labor law

✔ Personal injury law

✔ Real estate law

✔ Tax law

✔ Welfare law

Many large companies and government agencies need to be aware of different types of laws. For example, large corporations hire one attorney who specializes in copyright law, another who practices employment law, and a third whose focus is tax law. Paralegals, too, can specialize in a specific area such as tax law. The paralegal specializing in tax law assists the corporation in all legal matters relating to tax issues.

Growth Potential

The tasks assigned to a paralegal may vary depending on his or her education, training, and experience. Paralegals receive more responsibilities as their work experience increases. Also, employers supervise a paralegal less and less as his or her job performance improves. A paralegal who gains a great deal of experience within a company or government agency may advance to a supervisory or managerial level.

Questions to Ask Yourself

Which place of employment sounds most interesting to you? What areas of law interest you? Would you rather be a freelance paralegal? Would you like to manage or supervise a paralegal staff?

3

Life as a Paralegal

You could say I eat, drink, and sleep paralegal. I read Legal Assistant Journal *and* Paralegal *magazine, and spend my off hours at the law library. Even my closest friends are other paralegals. I love my job ... and my lifestyle.*

I wasn't good at anything in particular in school, but I loved organizing things. I get a real sense of satisfaction when I have finished something and it seems perfect. I also like to solve problems ... I get the same pleasure out of solving a problem as I do organizing something.

Coming out of high school, I thought about doing something law-related, but I wasn't sure what. My aunt is a lawyer, so I spent a few days with her while she was working. I got to know her assistant, Eric. He has worked for my aunt for six years. We talked about what it's like to be a paralegal, and something just clicked. Eric became my mentor, which is

There are many trade publications available that deal with issues of concern to lawyers and paralegals.

a person who can teach you all about an interesting career.

Eric said that after school, his first few years of paralegal work were tough. He said that he had to work much more than forty hours per week and that he did a lot of mind-numbing tasks. He is glad that he stuck it out, though, because now he oversees other paralegals at the firm and makes good money. He is also taking night classes and hopes to earn a law degree.

My first few years working as a paralegal weren't as tough as Eric's. I chose to work for one lawyer, so my hours weren't long—except right before a big case. I was also given more respon-sibility because there was only one other person on staff: the receptionist. I did do some mind-numbing tasks, but interesting tasks, like interviewing wit-nesses and finding out the facts of a case, made up for it.

Now I work for a large law firm. I love the work because I am always learning something new and getting paid for it! I have worked on cases that have made the news, which is exciting. My bosses closely supervised me when I first came here, but after proving myself, I've been given more to do with much less supervision. I have a laptop computer that I use for work, on which

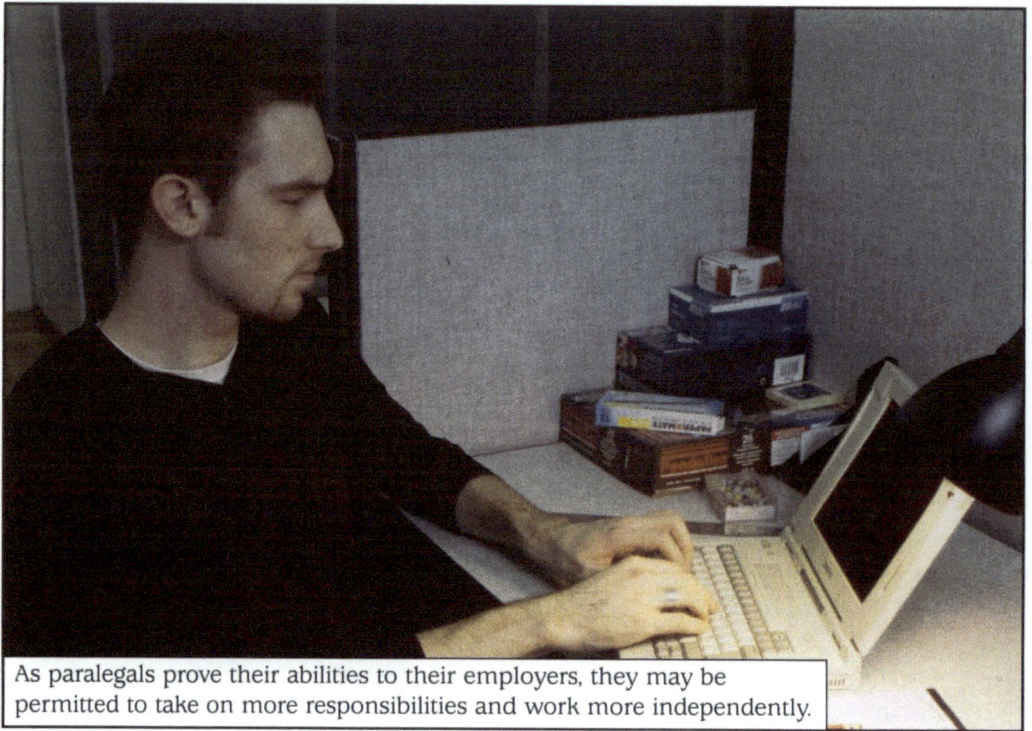

As paralegals prove their abilities to their employers, they may be permitted to take on more responsibilities and work more independently.

I organize my case and company files. I've even filled out legal forms for some of our cases over the Internet!
— Sharon, age twenty-four

As Eric's and Sharon's experiences demonstrate, working as a paralegal is not the same for everyone. Your education, abilities, interests, and training will affect your salary, workload, and future opportunities. The choices that you make today will impact your career as a paralegal.

Salaries

Paralegal salaries vary and are determined by a number of factors. Salaries depend on a person's education, training, and experience. Salaries also depend on the size, type, and location of the employer. Paralegals who work at large companies in large cities generally receive higher salaries than paralegals who work at small firms or in small towns.

Most established paralegals usually work forty hours per week and receive complete life and health insurance benefits. Most paralegals work year-round, but some paralegals work for only part of the year. This is because some employers hire paralegals during busy periods only. They pay temporary workers on an hourly basis.

A paralegal's average starting salary is approximately $21,000 per year. With five years' experience, this salary might increase to $32,000. A paralegal with ten or more years of experience can earn up to $40,000. Some paralegals can make as much as $90,000 yearly. In addition to salaries, over half of all working paralegals receive bonuses. The average yearly bonus is $2,000.

Paralegals working for the federal government can earn up to $40,000 per year. Paralegals working at the state or local level earn about $10,000 less. The average annual salary for law firm work is $30,000. As paralegals take on more responsibilities and receive more training, their salaries increase.

Building a Career

As a paralegal gains experience, he or she builds a career. The first years of paralegal employment differ from those that follow. As with most jobs, salaries increase and responsibilities expand over time.

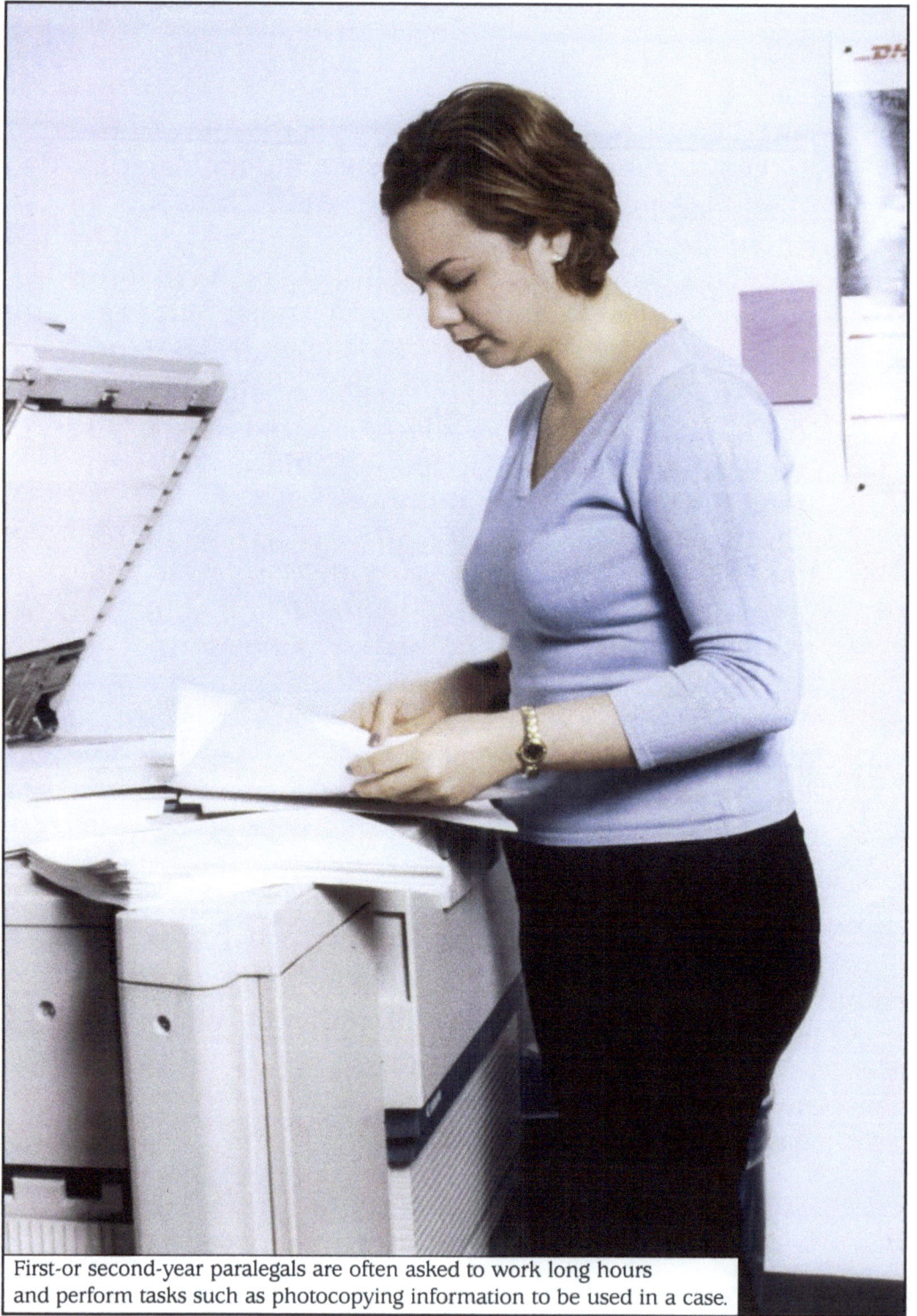

First-or second-year paralegals are often asked to work long hours and perform tasks such as photocopying information to be used in a case.

The First Two Years

During the first two years, paralegals discover which tasks they perform well and where they may need improvement. During these years, paralegals also improve their ability to complete tasks quickly and effectively. Most assignments during their first and second years test their ability to provide an employer with correct and careful research.

Employers often ask paralegals to work more than forty hours per week. They might even be asked to work as many as ninety hours in one week. Employers constantly supervise first- and second-year paralegals. Depending on where they work, paralegals might spend their days researching in a law library or photocopying information to be used in a case or for reports.

After Five Years

Since employers tend to supervise an experienced employee less closely, a paralegal will have much more responsibility and independence by the fifth year. Also, at this point, paralegals often decide which area of law most interests them. Corporate paralegals are often promoted to managing or supervising positions after five years. Some paralegals choose to leave their current employers and seek higher salaries and better positions.

Ten-Year Career

Even after working ten years as a paralegal, the challenges continue. In addition to their routine

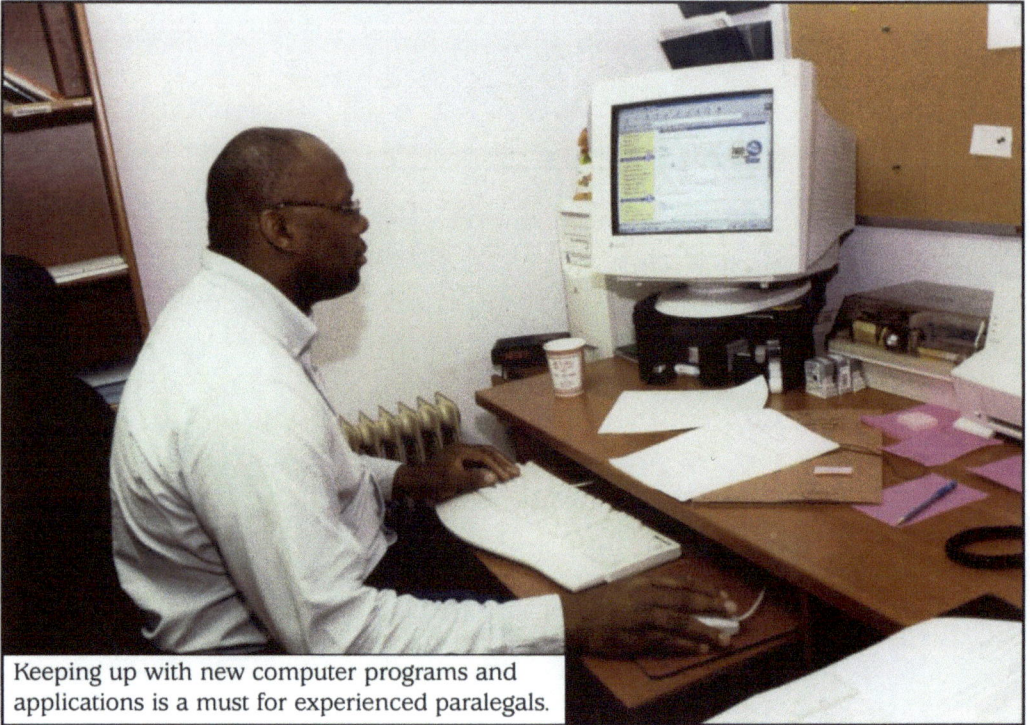
Keeping up with new computer programs and applications is a must for experienced paralegals.

tasks, paralegals must constantly remain informed of new laws and new interpretations of existing laws. They are also expected to be aware of new computer programs and applications. Understandably, employers give paralegals with ten years or more of experience a great deal of responsibility. These paralegals require little supervision.

A Career Change

Should a paralegal find himself or herself looking for a change, there are many options. A paralegal can apply his or her work experience to another job. A paralegal can become a lawyer. As a paralegal works closely with a lawyer, she or he can decide if practicing as an attorney is the next step.

Experience working as a paralegal also prepares you to work as:

✔ An occupational health and safety officer—Develops and writes health and safety plans for the workplace

✔ An insurance claims examiner—Examines the facts of an insurance claim that an individual or company has filed

✔ A patent agent—Helps individuals and companies obtain patents for ideas and products

✔ A title examiner—Researches the legal history of property or real estate

Questions to Ask Yourself

Does the career path of a paralegal sound like a rewarding one to you? Do you know anyone who could serve as a mentor for you? Have you asked your school counselor about finding a possible mentor in the paralegal profession?

4

Training to Become a Paralegal

Anyone interested in becoming a paralegal has several options. There are a number of ways to prepare. Different employers look for different qualifications. Some paralegal programs have more to offer than others. The best programs usually offer students job placement assistance upon graduation. It is also important to determine if a program offers internships. Internships are a valuable way for students to gain hands-on experience.

Most companies prefer to hire job applicants with some sort of formal paralegal training. There are both two- and four-year paralegal education programs. There is also a shorter certificate program. Some companies prefer to train employees on the job. They often hire high school or college graduates with no legal experience. They may also promote secretaries or clerks from within the company. Other companies hire people who have a particular type of experience, such as a background in tax preparation or health administration.

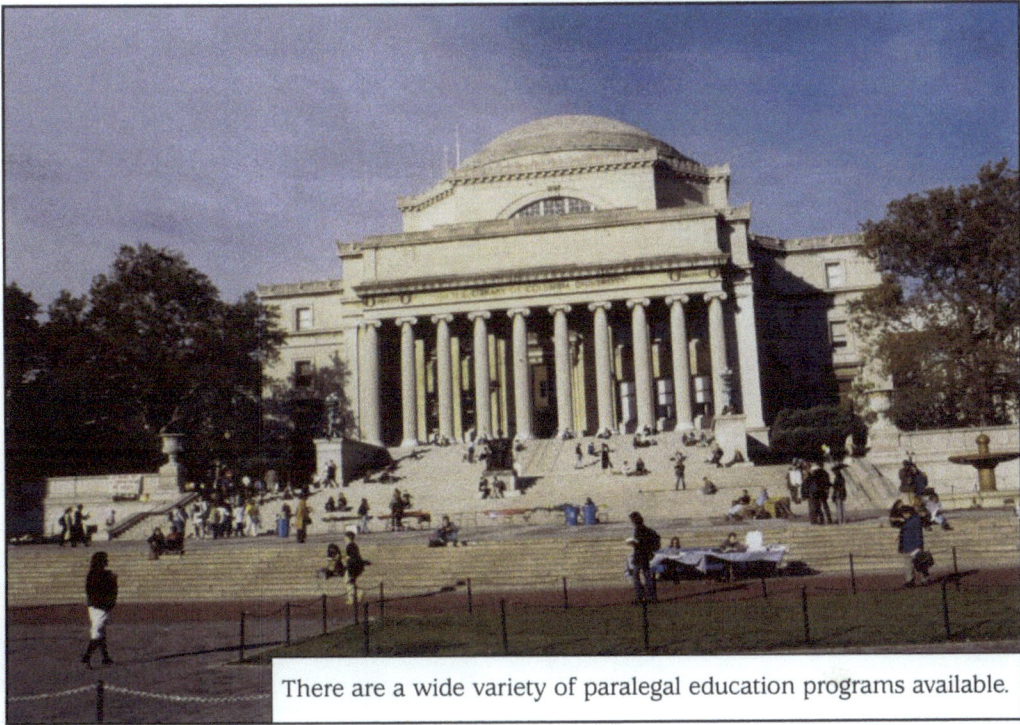

There are a wide variety of paralegal education programs available.

Education

It is estimated that there are 600 to 800 paralegal education programs or schools in the United States. The wide variety of paralegal education programs makes it possible for people of different backgrounds to become paralegals. Some schools or institutions that offer paralegal programs are:

- ✔ Community colleges
- ✔ Four-year colleges and universities
- ✔ Business colleges
- ✔ Privately owned institutions

Training Programs

Paralegals are asked to perform many different tasks. Because paralegal work is so wide-ranging,

The admissions requirements for paralegal education programs vary from school to school.

paralegal training varies slightly from school to school. The requirements for admission to these programs vary as well. Many schools or institutions simply require a high school diploma or an equivalent, while others accept only students with college degrees. Most programs offer part-time or night classes for students who work during the day. Overall, paralegal training programs fall into one of five basic categories:

✔ Two-year associate degree programs

✔ Four-year bachelor's degree programs

✔ Programs offered by private institutions

✔ Post-baccalaureate programs

✔ Master's degree programs

Two-Year Associate Degree Programs

An associate degree is awarded to a student who has completed two years of course work. Programs offering associate degrees can be found at many community colleges as well as four-year colleges. Required courses usually include subjects such as English and mathematics as well as paralegal courses. If a student is interested in continuing his or her education beyond the two years of study, he or she should make sure that credits from the two-year program will transfer to a four-year degree program.

Four-Year Bachelor's Degree Programs

Many colleges and universities offer paralegal education programs. A student who has completed four years of course work will receive a bachelor's degree. Course work includes studying subjects such as history, science, and mathematics, in addition to thirty-six semester units of paralegal course work. In this type of program, a student can major in paralegal studies and also take a variety of liberal arts courses.

Programs Offered by Private Institutions

Many private educational institutions offer short programs in paralegal training. These programs usually last from three to eighteen months. Upon completion, students receive a certificate. Many of these programs require that applicants have a high school diploma or GED, but they need not have attended college. Some students have already earned a two- or four-year degree at another college or university but lack specific paralegal training.

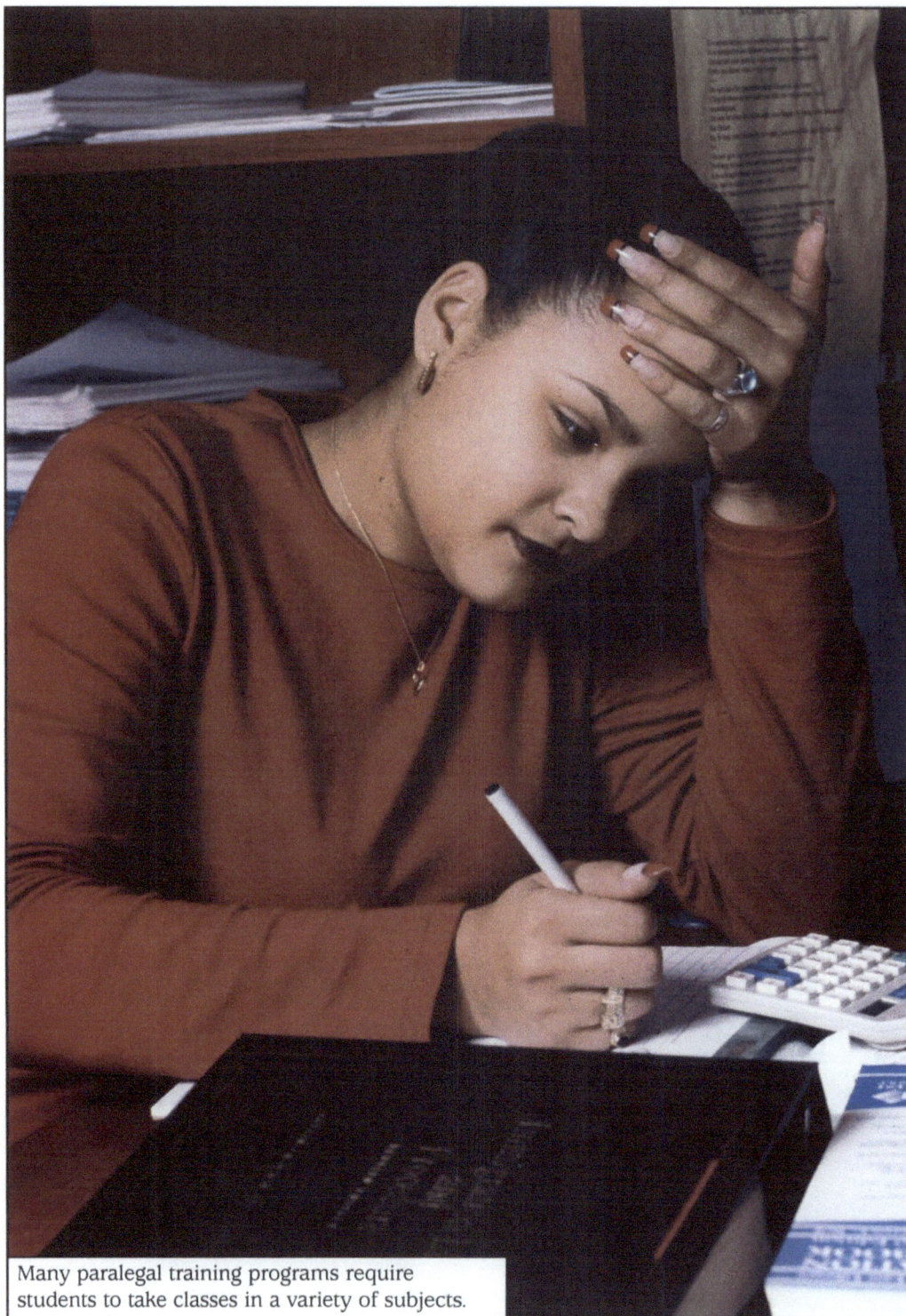
Many paralegal training programs require students to take classes in a variety of subjects.

Post-baccalaureate Programs

Similarly, a student who has earned his or her bachelor's degree at a four-year college or university may enroll in a paralegal certificate program. Most of these programs can be completed in one year or less. Students often find these courses offered at the college from which they earned their four-year degree.

Master's Degree Programs

Colleges and universities that offer two- and four-year paralegal programs sometimes offer advanced degrees in paralegal studies. Students must have already earned a bachelor's degree in order to participate in these programs.

Program Content

Paralegal programs vary from school to school. Many programs require that students attend classes such as English and mathematics in addition to paralegal courses. Most paralegal course work, however, varies little from program to program. This course work includes but is not limited to:

✔ An introductory paralegal course, which discusses the law and the paralegal field

✔ Litigation (law suit) or civil procedure

✔ Legal research and writing

✔ Legal ethics

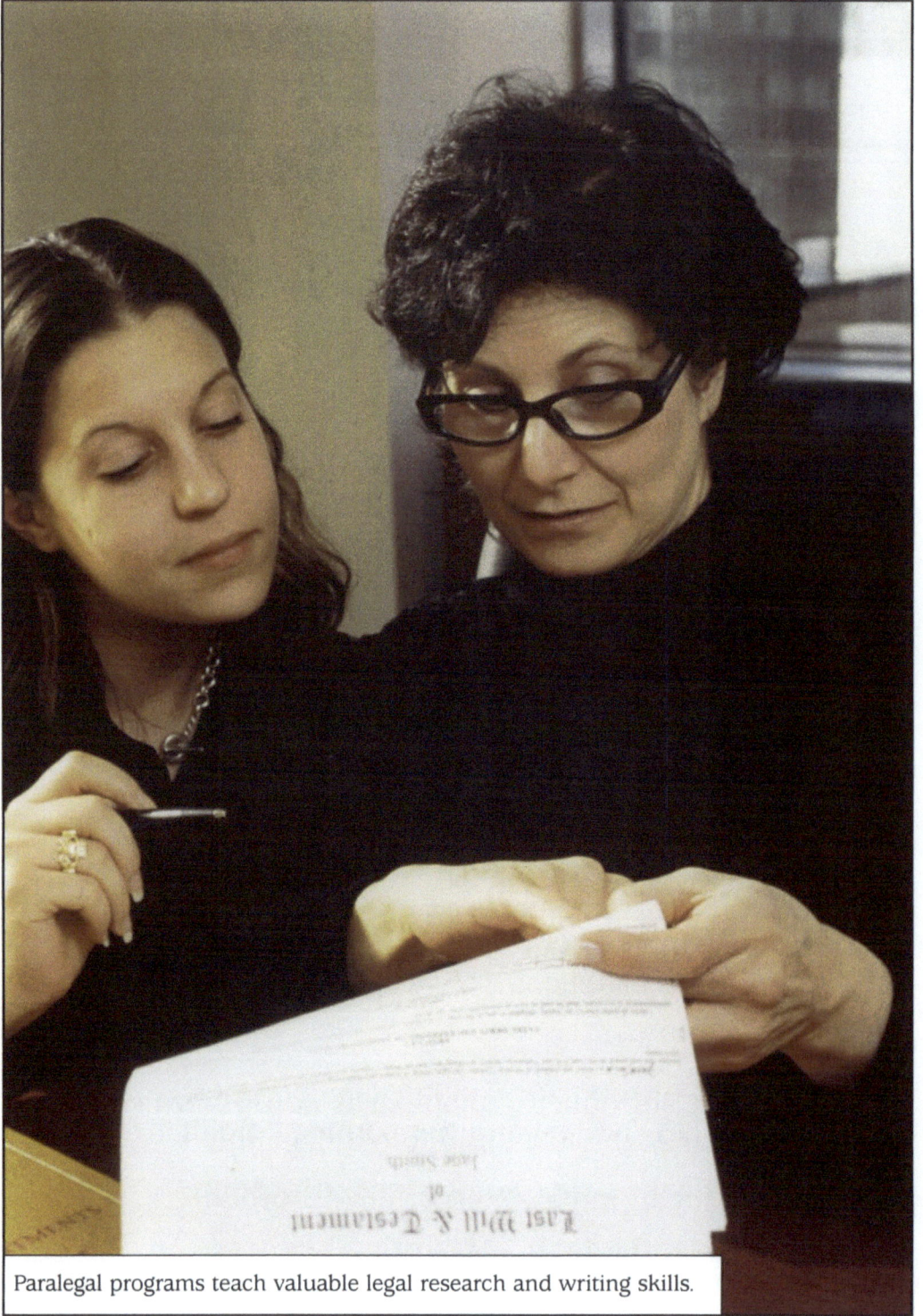

Paralegal programs teach valuable legal research and writing skills.

In addition, schools may offer specialized programs, such as:

- ✔ Family law
- ✔ Business and corporate law
- ✔ Wills, trusts, and estate planning
- ✔ Real property/real estate transactions
- ✔ Taxation
- ✔ Bankruptcy
- ✔ Contracts
- ✔ Commercial law
- ✔ Computer applications for legal assistants

After I graduated from high school, I really didn't know what I wanted to do. My parents suggested that I attend the local college, but I really just wanted to start working and get my own place. I found a job with a friend of mine at a department store. I earned enough money to get my own little apartment and I was pretty happy.

After a while at the store, I began wishing that my job was a little more challenging. A friend of mine had recently enrolled in a paralegal program at the local college. She seemed really excited about it and suggested that I enroll as well.

I didn't know anything about law, and I didn't really know what being a paralegal was about. I also didn't want to quit working. So I figured that in order to afford school I would either have to take out huge loans or move back in with my parents. Neither idea appealed much to me.

My friend explained to me that she took her courses at night, and that rather than having to go to college for four years, she was getting an associate degree, which would take only two years. That idea sounded more appealing to me, but I still didn't understand what a paralegal did. I asked my friend to explain. After she explained it, it sounded neat.

She was excited to start her career and had just started an internship with a local law firm, which she was enjoying. She said her internship involved interesting work, and she was helping a paralegal do research for an upcoming case. I finally decided to find out more about the paralegal course at the college, and liking what I heard, I enrolled the next semester.

I still work at the store during the day, which is great because I get to keep my apartment. But now I have something more. Every night I go to class and learn about all sorts of legal issues, which I find very interesting and challenging. I am also excited to start my own internship soon. I arranged to get the time off from work. Sure, I'll make a little less money, but soon I'll graduate and be able to start a whole new career.

—Elsie, age nineteen

5

Getting Started

The type of education you choose can affect your career options. The right training will offer you the best chance for success in the world of paralegal work. Before you look into schools or programs, have a clear idea of your goals. Knowing your goals will help you determine which type of training program is right for you.

Finding Paralegal Schools or Programs

Several sources can help you find a school or program. You can ask:

✔ Your high school counselor

✔ Local universities or colleges

✔ Local law firms that rely on paralegal assistance

✔ Local bar associations

Your high school guidance counselor can help you find a paralegal education program that's right for you.

Paralegal organizations can also help you find schools and programs. Paralegal associations assist the paralegal work force. Through these associations, paralegals share knowledge and experience. These organizations also set the educational and training standards for paralegals.

A few of these organizations have developed rating systems for paralegal schools and programs. For a school or program to receive such an organization's approval, they must meet certain standards. The American Bar Association and the American Association of Paralegal Education offer approval ratings for paralegal schools and programs. Other paralegal associations are listed in the For More Information section of this book.

Choosing a School or Program

In addition to finding out if a school or program has received the approval of a paralegal association, you should consider the following points.

Reputation

Finding a school or program with a solid reputation, one that is known for providing its students with a good education, is important. Ask people in the legal field or school counselors to recommend high quality schools and programs. You might also speak with students who attend or have attended a school or program that interests you.

Mission

When people create programs or schools, they have a goal, or mission, in mind. They also write a goal or mission statement. The mission statement outlines what the school or program hopes to do for its students and the community. You can usually find a program's or school's mission statement in its general information pamphlet. You can also ask a representative of the school or program to explain its goal or mission.

Graduation or Certification Requirements

You should find out what types of classes and how many classes you will need to attend in order to graduate or become certified. Some schools or programs emphasize that students receive a general liberal arts education as well as a paralegal education. These schools and programs will prepare you well for the world of paralegal work.

Faculty Backgrounds

Your professors, teachers, or instructors should have proper educational credentials as well as paralegal or legal training. They should have an understanding of what employers expect from a paralegal. Your teachers should have a strong background in the specific subject or subjects they teach. Also, check to see if the school or program has a full-time or part-time staff. Full-time staff members are usually more available to students than those who work part-time.

There are many factors to consider when selecting a paralegal education program.

Classes and Curriculum

It is important that a program or school provides students with a thorough paralegal education. Students should study legal theory or law and learn paralegal job skills. The program or school curriculum is the set of courses you need to complete in order to become a trained paralegal. Your courses should teach you how to understand legal research and writing. You should also have an opportunity to study and discuss ethics, or professional standards of conduct. The curriculum should be geared to help students develop necessary skills such as good communication, problem solving, organization, computer literacy, and critical thinking.

Student Services

A good school or program will offer students additional services, such as orientation for new students, counseling, financial aid, career development, and tutoring. The school or institution should inform students of important legal organizations and associations. Staff should be able to direct students interested in further education to schools with more advanced programs. Also, be sure that the school or institution offers job placement assistance to graduating students.

Student Resources

Students should have access to a law library and computers. Look for a school or institution that offers classes that are small in size. It should also offer a secure environment and be accessible to those with disabilities.

Student Activities

Schools or institutions should help students find internships. Internships, which can be paid or unpaid, provide students with valuable on-the-job experience. Students should also have opportunities to do volunteer work or join honor societies or clubs.

Training from Home

Some schools and programs offer students the option of taking classes from home. In addition to the considerations already discussed, think about the following:

✔ Are you able to work well on your own, to be your own motivator?

✔ Do you have the self-discipline to get things done independently?

✔ What method would you use to take a class—mail, television or video broadcasts, the Internet?

✔ How many interactions would you have with instructors?

✔ When and how would that interaction take place?

Credentials

A credential is a title. It certifies that a person has met certain standards. A few professional paralegal organizations have developed exams.

Paralegals who meet certain requirements are allowed to take the exams. If the paralegal passes the exam, the organization certifies that he or she is a highly qualified paralegal. After passing the exam, a paralegal can add the credential to his or her name and résumé.

Paralegals who pass the exam given by the National Association of Legal Assistants become certified legal assistants. They may place the credential "CLA" after their names. A paralegal who passes the exam given by the National Federation of Paralegal Associations becomes a registered paralegal. The exam is called the Paralegal Advanced Competency Exam, or PACE for short. The paralegal is allowed to place the credential "RP" or "PACE Registered Paralegal" after her or his name. The credential shows employers that the paralegal has taken an extra step to prove his or her abilities.

A Bright Future

The paralegal field is growing rapidly. Experts predict that the profession will continue to grow during the next decade. This means that more schools and programs will offer paralegal classes.

One of the best ways to start your career as a paralegal is to visit the job placement office at your school. You might also consider attending paralegal association meetings. These associations also maintain lists of job openings.

A paralegal with a strong educational background or a lot of on-the-job experience will move ahead quickly. With the heavy use of computers in legal work, employers prefer to hire job candidates with solid computer skills. Also, employers look for applicants who have had experience working as an intern in a law office.

Questions to Ask Yourself

Do you want to attend a school or program close to your home? Do you want to attend classes during the day or at night? Do you want to attend school on a full-time or part-time basis? Do you want a credential? Are there paralegal organizations in your area that can help you choose a school or training?

Glossary

associate degree   A two-year degree consisting of general education courses as well as a specialized area of study.

attorney   Also called a lawyer, a person who is trained, educated, and licensed to act as a legal agent.

bachelor's degree   A four-year degree consisting of a major area of study as well as a base of general education courses.

certificate   A document stating that a person has completed a course of study.

copyright law   Laws relating to copyrights, or protection of an idea or object.

corporation   An association or organization that legally acts as one unit.

credential   A title showing that a person has met a certain standard.

criminal law   Laws relating to criminals or law breakers.

curriculum   The course of studies that one pursues while earning a degree or certificate.

employment law   Laws relating to working.

ethics   Knowing right from wrong.

family law   Laws relating to family matters.

health care law   Laws relating to health or medical matters.

housing law   Laws relating to landlord/tenant and home issues.

labor law   Laws relating to work issues.

law   An established regulation or rule of conduct.

lawyer   Also called an attorney, a person who is trained, educated, and licensed to act as a legal agent.

litigation   Lawsuit.

paralegal   A person who has specific education, training, or work experience that allows him or her to assist a lawyer in legal matters.

real estate law   Laws relating to real estate and property issues.

tax law   Laws relating to tax issues.

welfare law   Laws relating to government welfare issues.

WƏW

For More Information

In the United States

American Association for Paralegal Education
2965 Flowers Road South, Suite 105
Atlanta, GA 30341
(770) 452-9877
Web site: http://www.aafpe.org

American Bar Association
Standing Committee on Legal Assistants
541 N. Fairbanks Ct.
Chicago, IL 60611
(312) 988-5522
Web site: http://www.abanet.org/legalassts

Association of Legal Administrators
175 East Hawthorn Parkway, Suite 325
Vernon Hills, IL 60061-1428
(847) 816-1212
Web site: http://www.alanet.org

Legal Assistant Management Association
2965 Flowers Road South, Suite 105
Atlanta, GA 30341
(770) 457-7746
Web site: http://www.lamanet.org

National Association of Legal Assistants
1516 South Boston Avenue, Suite 200
Tulsa, OK 74119
(918) 587-6828
Web site: http://www.nala.org

National Federation of Paralegal Associations
P.O. Box 33108
Kansas City, MO 64114-0108
(816) 941-4000
Web site: http://www.paralegals.org

The United States government's official Web site
    for jobs and employment information
Web site: http://www.usajobs.opm.gov

In Canada

The Canadian Bar Association
902-50 O'Connor Street
Ottawa, ON K1P 6L2
(613) 237-2925, (613) 237-1988,
(800) 267-8860
e-mail: info@cba.org
Web site: http://www.cba.org

Inter Canada Credit
181 Main Street West, #C-117
Hamilton, ON L8P 4S1
(888) 738-7277
e-mail: icc@netinc.ca
Web site: http://home.netinc.ca/ ~ icc/icc.htm

For Further Reading

Davis, Mary Lee. *Working in Law and Justice* (Exploring Careers). Minneapolis, MN: Lerner Publishing Group, 1999.

Fox, Ken. *Everything You Need to Know About Your Legal Rights.* New York: Rosen Publishing Group, 1998.

Frost-Knappman, Elizabeth, Edward W. Knappman, and Lisa Paddock, eds. *Courtroom Drama: 120 of the World's Most Notable Trials.* Farmington Hills, MI: Visible Ink Press, 1997.

Goodrich, David Lee. *The Basics of Paralegal Studies.* Upper Saddle River, NJ: Prentice Hall College Division, 2000.

LeValliant, Ted, and Marcel Theroux. *What's the Verdict? You're the Judge in 90 Tricky Courtroom Quizzes.* New York: Sterling Publications, 1991.

Morton, Joyce. *Legal Office Procedures.* Upper Saddle River, NJ: Prentice Hall, 2000.

Schneeman, Angela. *Paralegal Ethics.* Albany, NY: Delmar Publishing, 2000.

Wirths, Claudine G. *Choosing a Career in Law Enforcement.* New York: Rosen Publishing Group, 1997.

WᴥW

Index

About the Author

Holly Cefrey is a freelance writer and researcher. She has written a wide variety of historical, medical, and self-help books for the young adult market. She attended the University of Nebraska before moving to New York.

Photo Credits

Cover by Antonio Mari. All interior shots by Antonio Mari except p. 2 © FPG International; pp. 8, 20, 24 © Corbis; p. 22 © The Everett Collection.

Layout

Geri Giordano

www.ingramcontent.com/pod-product-compliance
Lightning Source LLC
Chambersburg PA
CBHW042059210326
41597CB00045B/84